ORDINARY SUN

Ordinary Sun

by Matthew Henriksen

Black Ocean
Boston - New York - Chicago

Black Ocean
P.O. Box 52030
Boston, MA 02205
blackocean.org

ISBN 978-0-9844752-2-3

Library of Congress Cataloging-in-Publication Data

Henriksen, Matthew.
 Ordinary sun / Matthew Henriksen. -- 1st ed.
    p. cm.
 ISBN 978-0-9844752-2-3
 I. Title.
 PS3608.E56455O73 2011
 811'.6--dc22
                                    2010046986

FIRST EDITION

ACKNOWLEDGEMENTS

Thanks to the editors of the following journals, where poems from *Ordinary Sun* originally appeared: *Absent, Agriculture Reader, Art Amiss, Coconut, The Cultural Society, Fascicle, Forklift Ohio, Free Verse, Front Porch Journal, H_NGM_N, Handsome, horse less review, Indiana Review, Kulture Vulture, Lit, MiPoesias, Poemeleon, Sink Review, Third Coast, This Recording,* and *Tight.* Poems in the sections "The Talk" and "Is Holy" appeared in the chapbook *Is Holy* by horse less press in August, 2006.

"Gorge" borrows the sentence "All answers are hells" from Fanny Howe's novel *The Deep North.*

Thanks, for assistance with these poems or other poetry matters, to Tom Andes, Andrea Baker, Phil Cordelli, Julia Cohen, Lucile Fessler, Kate Greenstreet, Jane Gregory, Ben Mazer, Joyelle McSweeney, Keith Newton, Sam King, Mitch Taylor, Tony Tost, and Jared White. Thanks to Carrie Olivia Adams and Janaka Stucky for publishing this book. Thanks to my teachers Gerald Saindon, Karl Elder, Michael Heffernan, James Whitehead and Brian Wilkie, and to Charles O'Donnell and Don Choffel at the Dickson Street Bookshop. Whiskey to the heart for Adam Clay and Shannon Jonas. Eternal gratitude and love to the Henriksen and Widder families and to Pete Panopoulos.

for Katy and Adele

TABLE OF CONTENTS

Here is unfenced existence:
Facing the sun, untalkative, out of reach.

—Philip Larkin

Copse

An eye is not enough.
A hand rubs an unpainted fence.

Foreground of bees,
helicopters in weeds.

I connived with moss
on the corner of the garage.

Robins contained the hedges.
Trampled grass claimed the lawn.

We lived in a small house
in the quiet North.

In a clearing between
a copse of elms and the river
conniving grew a shape.

We found light in a jar under the elms.

We drank at night and ran across the dam.
Nathan climbed down and stood in the river.

We broke into the lock station and threw
cinder blocks down the flood chamber.

I only asked for a beginning
in a blade chamber,

a shower of bees
in a cinder's slam.

Waking to whiteness and unsure
who is there,

the shape in the cloth,
my dove and blisters.

The voice inside a jar sings anthems in the field.
The openness of that place expands backwardly.

Immediacy pushes
what I gather apart.

What I cannot find in the morning is most myself.

She stood atop the ravine above
where I was beyond repair.

Vines tangled
up the crags,

fingers, hair,
history as war,
the helicopter's sigh.

She stood
there
to say "aberration,"
to want the day back.

There were days I climbed the hill
and rested, though I've outgrown
sleeping on the ravine's scarred side.

I woke on the carpet, opened
the patio door and stared.
A swallow flew in and perched.

I've grown out of
that sort of miracle.

From above the tracks she offered
bees as blessing and pestilence,
history as war, tongue as blade.

I lived lovely in a cut, day-long buzzing.

A shift of clouds
and the floor dull as knives,

it was all right when I could look
at the sky, but when your friend
brought me in to look at the table

made of bees, I could see
where knife-gnaws never healed.

Another man's table saddens beyond bees.

It's over, I began, and asked for the storm
to hold off.

The room could not go
beyond the flap

of blinds flipping in light
and light, quiet wind.

I only asked for objects played against
what held there.

The wind grew old in its hive,
too old to produce negatives
below the cinder block:

swallows above dogwood
and apple blossoms above

traffic in an old town square,
whorls on a finger.

I threw rocks into the river,
acorns at the fence, heard

a whisper, fingered the lip
of an open jar and in

that whisper turned
a swallow, asleep.

Hard to remember not to fight
especially the worst things
and read everything with sympathy.

She stood atop the ravine
above puddles by the tracks.

I heard her on a fingertip
inside a jar. I got home
and smashed a glass.

I don't know what to judge.

Waking to whiteness and unsure
who is there, the shape in the cloth,

my dove and blisters
stunned beyond sunlight,

the hive moving, inside
almost complete, a lighthouse

on an island, one eye.
I know light doesn't see.

What we don't know is our only law.

In a copse Nathan found a jar of bees.
To hold "aberration" we must climb down
one ravine into another.

We got out of the car.
We set our bodies in the grass.
Stones held our breath.

Is Holy

REGULATIONS OF THE ASSASSINS

Farcers told me I went to extremes,
so I went to live in the extreme.

Seldom did I return but to twitch as a twig in the scene.
Call your memory finger and point the place unmapped.

Interior wings pout over the river indentured to Earth's bend.
Horizon to scold the tongues down. The golden bed of torture.

A foothold in the mundane shell disclaimed veins.
Never again became a rip, a mole's undoing, a hawk's cry.

In all that nonsense I became a gun.
It's raining now, goddamn.

AFTERLIFE ON A LONG, SHALLOW HILL

The footed rhyme of grave
gained this cobbler's shrine

benign in grass, this body, alive,
as in a moving cloud, a sun.

And when. Or not when but of. Of longing.
After the night unglues it's unknown anyway. Then o.

Oblivion's lens never closes. Diner won't blink.
Its song demolishes our total losses.

People were terrified, then gone.
The soil opened its skin, hatching poppies.

AFTERLIFE WITH STILL LIFE

The glass has not been broken.
A rest is a favor to the knee

at the crest of the ocean waters
about to recede with the crabs, the white

on their backs, shadows like glass,
what reflection looks through.

Your skull is
perfecting the triangle,

making nothing out of three.
Another makes immaculate the mind.

AFTERLIFE ENDING AS A QUESTION

The world began in wrong. The clouds
prove this by their leniency. As grace

disturbs our sentiment for violence
so the bush lays its ambush of lilacs.

The shortness of the fuse is what
we must suppose God meant
for us to love. Let all songs

shorten the fuse, then
defuse it.

What is love but a negative collaboration?

MOTIONLESS

Heard the well cry, "Brothers." And the orchard answer,
"An arm of wind twists in a bed sheet of leaves."

Heard another brother cry back,
"The moon is a sack of spider eggs."

Heard a dried out sandal say,
"The moon is where the dead

don't live either." Heard from a ghost,
"When the moon shines down into the well,

horses rake hell of sleep, roof behooved
with beating and pawing, voices reaching skin."

APPLETON, WISCONSIN

Held immaculately by tunes of lawnmowers and metal chains,
an avenue lined with withered clippings and weeds preceded wrong.

Filth congregated endlessly in miniature disasters, broken
twigs and crushed anthills, sweepings arranged to vanish.

When people lied, the stars came back enjoyably,
though they contrived to burn them, and sang hymns.

It was as if the world echoed from a well.
I shouted, "All parables lead to hierarchy."

This is terrible to admit.
Speaking backwardly has no limit.

PARKWAY & BENNETT

The houses darkened quietly
as if the edges had been rained on.

A welt of light remained
behind a hedge

at the corner house
where the mannequin stood.

That was my crazy family you saw.
That was our grass that looked burned.

Those were the screams
of our happiness you mistook.

GROVES

I woke in a grove to a crack of gunfire that seemed without distance.

The peach trees meant to melt under the sky,
which was the pale phantom of every sky I knew.

I questioned my arrival with the authority of amnesia.
Surely, one before me had scratched questions in the bark.

I tried to hold on to my rapport with nonsense,
knowing there was nothing I wished to know,

each morning an illumination of what abides,
each morning condensing the sounds I'd loved,

I suppose, as a wolf loves bleating things,
though supposition demands hunger

and the dry throat going blank.
I knew the shallow hill of pines and the woodman

crunching pinecones, gun slung, trudging
through the thoughtless openness of that place,

every seed already named, yet the air in blankets
shadowed over motives which took root invisibly,

or had so in mind. I had so many groves I proposed
my own, regrettable, a wish to pass through a rainstorm.

I slipped along the road, all I knew of this grove,
with rain like insects translucent in the headlights.

Where my mind gripped the road I belonged.
Fear grew wings in the rain. The mind was built to myth.

I flew upon the winds for the dead to know my name.
My eyes unlocked to a waning pasture beyond the grove.

I drove among the living and the dead as objects
waking together on the bed of an unwaking stream.

The Talk

AN ANGEL'S GENDER DESCRIBES RESEMBLANCE TO

I came up with this tangent casting a gentle
ripple that did not disturb the ducks,

their familial syntax, their taxonomies, sentences
whispered to the boy in such a way that he could not hear,

though he sat in the boat with me. Really creepy, he would
have thought, but I don't give these assignations

to anyone but you, these constant convolutions
in which we sulk and confer, my unconscious, invited guest.

Your presence would terrify the boy or bore
his grimacing wit to another sip of Pepsi

from the can he eyed in the bait shop after a gaze full
of chubs and crawdads, the worms' carton communities,

and on the wall the polished muskellunge with breathing scales
that he went to touch, until you flashed in its eye

a demonstrative "Noli me tangere," another
unnamable face the boy must face

without a mask, the honeyed words, and the winged ships of lies.

AN ANGEL HUNG BY HER HAIR HARKENS THE MUSIC OF HARP-LIKE FLESH

The boy will love this angel with ethereal carnality
and in such an inconclusive circus

inherit the folly of prescient ironic wit,
if you can imagine scaffolding ad infinitum.

But I won't imagine it because, as I will tell the boy,
even when she hangs there we can see the cornucopia

of her breast, the she-shell, the shield of her booby
shouting "à nous, la liberté," though she stops breathing

with the scales of justice tomorrow, armored lizard shrieking "now."

AN ANGEL UNLEARNS THE LIBEL OF EXHILARATION

I once took the boy to a movie about bicycles.
He fell in love with bicycles.

He fell upon his bicycle, and from. Upon
the thorns, he bled. He learned

his lesson not to learn. The elocution
of the vine evinced the fastened module

of esoteric remonstration. So he blew
his nose and made roses of his cheeks.

So the coward died, who lost his
bicycle. Forever turning, the

desecrating never ends. Amen.

ANGELS GIVE BIRTH AT SANITIZED ALTARS

Had I but time enough, boy, and a world to ravage

beyond the thick knots of my own blood,
she'd have me on the hood of the Honda

and conceive a horse. Or so I would say to the boy,
if he would understand the hoof unlocks itself from age to age,

and that an old man's feet molt, wrappings of memory
shed so distance may approach the skin.

Only the old man can recognize his own hooves,
though they've gone and he's too tired to see how funny that is.

Therefore, boy, I could say, you're screwed in your unscrewing
and too busy with your fuss to notice the blistery mess you leave.

Disgusting, the boy would think, but won't,
because I leave him to his sofa bucking

and run the streets bashing my heels on the concrete until
I hear them clop.

THE ONLY ANGEL IS THE ANGLE
OF DELIVERANCE

If a boy leaves by train at a volatile speed
he will kill a man on his Sunday morning drive.

These circumstances are arbitrary and certain,
as the forecast always gets it wrong.

Such is going down the mountain,
the roof, the slanted rain: the friction

of the isosceles that is half the friction
of a pair of wings that would lead the boy

upward from the wreckage, though for
now it's the other half the boy wants,

the sinking flame flagging under.

WENT DOWN TO THE RIVER, THAT ANGEL

The boy's symbolic acquisitions equate to a rhyme

representing the quantitative semblance between fishes and birds,
if you catch my drift. Could only the boy read signs.

In other words, the boy's cognizance is
breeched at the abortion of daylight,

static nightscape stillborn on the neighborhood's lawns,
an oozy frieze of potential memory.

And beat off. Cried, "Azure, behold me! I belong to the sky."

There's a numinous ring that's been bled clean
and found allergenic, the mainstream disaster of our era,

a doorway to the peephole into the girl's locker room
where the fortitude's innocence meets the laundry of indulgence.

His sister screams. So the boy dreams azure is blue is sky
and nightfall not a verbosity of electrocution.

THE FRONT LAWN IS THE PASTURE
AN ANGEL RESTS UPON

A head. Noting, like the sun, the boy
nods off. And off is the sound

clicking to rectify the posture of polyphony
in his penitent reluctance to fake oblation.

Dear Heaven, the yard is full of moths
I'd beseech him to love, to consecrate with obsequious dotage.

To harness-relegate. To emulsify with rhubarb.
To begin with narrative and end in the spasmodic demonology

of the forest, from whence angels hail
amorous petunias at forgiveness.

THE ANGEL HAD A HEAD, AND NAMED THE HEAD "TACITURNITY"

Trying to tell the boy magnifies his disastrous
manifestations of the abyss. For example,

his laundry has coalesced with his dishes,
mortifying the fishes, deranging their semantics.

What is an idiom to an idiot child
the boy prefigures with contortions
of want, his appendages on the baseball field.

Clover is a symbol of loss, a bat
the rector of acquiescence, chain-link fencing
the petrified governess of the shield.

Liberty is pretended by insects
mitigating in the furnace of discovery.

Sometimes I concede the boy has a lip for mercy.

I DREAMED THE ANGEL WAS A HORSE WITH HER EYES CLOSED

Fornication grows ordinary, boy, when it appears on
television. Nearing oppression, the meek shall disinherit

their mirth unto the lowliest of dawdlers in dresses of
mildew along the edges of the Seine where the blinking taxi-man

winks boldly in repetition at maidens of infiltration,
their hostels coffins, the mold around their eyes, yes,

antibody to lust—they begin to sing.

THE LAST ANGEL IS TATTOOED "BUTTRESS"

The boy, of course, is the last to learn that the girl has done

herself in. Spontaneity led to combustion of
the unctuous bust. In such a state, and is the state, the state

of air is stone. Fabled, florescence turned to ash
and the ashes glowed, starry to the dirt.

There it was, through his fingers, the earth
an eternity. It made the fires cold.

Mine of Losses

GHOST

Heaven must subject itself to the city for

the city to lose function. A throng of sparrows
and one gutter pipe must be all that sing.

The multitudes wilt from their professions and,
thus, professing. Hollyhocks taking in light are merciless.

God dreamed a professor of cinema saw the final image
on the last lost reel to Satan's Nightmares.

No one deemed God safe after that.
He took to wandering Brooklyn

with aimless pleasure, looking for
bridges to cross: crossing, and returning.

He'd lost his desperation, and without it
how could civilization admire itself?

This was the beginning of the third year
no one called for anyone. So it is writ.

THE FAITH

God slept in the galleys and woke in the Streets of Paradise,
then prefabricated rapture to deliver the distressed.

Whispered alleys dawned on the hill-ruptured sunset
an admonished coin sang.

Such as when the dogs are sick
and the body craves incisions on the ear.

Distressed birds
hazarding grace
stopped to walk.

NEW SPARROW , NEW SORROW

Moon burnt up in a tree limb's wobble.
Heaven's sort of nimble.

Not to want the origin of light, to want its myth.
To want the stroke across the jaw without the fist.

Walked among unplotted ways.
Made maps to joy. Waited near birds.

Liked haloed fury made of things.
Foraged through the brain, begot a bird.

Her throat nestled in a lion's jaw,
her heart the throb about.

Say stars, said the image,
then climbed into a blink

splayed amid the eyelids
and places eyelids made.

PRAYER

In a field of yes, a hole amid the asters,
a crow feels the weight of asking.

A crow feels ageless.
The faster spinning still frames

burgeoning nonsense offering
cloudless marrow burning stones.

YARD WORK

The whisper lasted several hours in the blade chamber,

and the bleeding slowed. That Saturday
was the longest and now it's over.

When you come back, I'll
be behind the barn stacking

sticks again, singing
"stay, stay, stay,"

damn bones, bird
bones, brain-boned

mocking song leaking light along a sheaf of lawn,
razor-clipped answer to a nonce prayer.

EITHER ETHER OR

Set down her ax
to scrutinize the chopping block.

Far from the field
the sun sang out

a bucket of tallow,
yellow pallor—
light aging in a glass.

Branches and twigs
hinged on thorns:

divine the drunken
master of form.

Her axe made flowers open.

Returning to the kitchen
she was born in, the ax

outside the window,
was that her standing

in the doorway and
the house unfolding?

Birds beyond the window cried the glass.

The yard was a song at each edge,
and all's edges edging.

AS THE NUDE COMPOSITE WISHES FOR HEAT WITHOUT VIOLENCE

I wept lost amid the wallpaper's mimicked
church garden. I taught harmonies to wires.

The buzzing grew less distant and implied
the complicity of the whole belongs

to the choked mouth's consent.
A box goes on forever. Set on a rail,

a box becomes a sky. There's a blanket
underground, I understand.

Constellations froze on the eye of the dog
chained to the metal post I hammered home.

RESOLUTION

The drift of horses magnifies the dust of dusk.
An owl condoles the house with a loud retch.

I made a whisper to make her body blink.
Her fingers rooted upon unnamable waste.

Her spine wound like a spire out
of time, contorted unclimbably.

A sickness grew out of my love, so I loved her sickness
and spoke in terms to make it grow.

I grew sick of repetition and so my love.
My love fell into the sickness of her well.

I fashioned a bower to keep out birds.
I feigned company and spoke in shades.

Pretending to hear her, I cried, "Invisible sky."
I begged her back but brambles she became.

I shooed the last blackbird from her limbs
and brushed the snow from her torso.

IN THE MEADOW AT THE PARTING
OF THE WAYS

All the buckets wanted us to wail the day away.
We did not become like light on the foothill

while the cars sped past.
We did not become that.

We sat with our buckets and talked about the radiator.
We left our words in plain sight on the hood of the car.

We did not hear the rabbit rustle.
A thorn turned out to be a moth.

We talked too much about everything.
A trembling glass rubbed all the leaves at once.

The day grew a geometry
of words, shades to hold the daylight back.

COLD FOLLIES

The sky sews itself to highness,
the post of patrician.

A practitioner of blindness speaks toward God.
Then God touches the Word,
scales fish in our sleep.

The sea gains against cold motion.
Hoped for like mud
torn bunting and blankets haunt these fair grounds.

God steps out of self to smoke,
is smoke, thinks this funeral
parlor of moles, hacks
their aching, speaks
their resistance.

Who is left to kill?

Mother stalking the playground howling scores,
raw umbrage, spare parts, gunstocks
glitter last.

Corolla in the Midden

I

Not too drunk to mistake
the white blotch for dog kill

under a streetlight above some trees,
nor to walk through the ghost

of what never lived or left a body
to haul away, I continue

to breathe imperfectly perfect air
I don't dance through.

I just cross the street and cross out
the thought, but keep the mess

stranger lovers told me I don't deserve
or deserve. So, that is something

to start out from, with the dog's nose
obscure in tulips, sniffing another dog's dung,

real dung and a fake mouth,
where the world works out

what the world will between
fuel and flash, as shape

precedes color, the Greek said,
but not on this lawn

without chemicals and rich down
in that city dirt. Each leaf denies

another nightmare in its scent.
I am not conjuring

but curl my eye's arms around
these tree tops and trees in the past

and do not embark. Everywhere
is past, and I passed longing

when I nearly stepped on a snake
on a sidewalk at the bottom of a hill.

Under the yellow-amber spent bulb
the snake's skin looked like worm skin.

I see this kind of shit
often but not more often than I like.

Far gone, I need a poison shiver
out of the shapeless mind

to find out where I live, to make up
a place to sleep.

When I don't sleep I can sleep
with crickets, or trucks,

or the names of our dead.
Harmony has taught me to stop loving

because the most disfigured eye
swells with love with

or without seeing the mangled face.
I can have more empathy for a dog

than a child and have no empathy
for you, only a disfigured grace to strike

your notions to smoke until
we have between us

only motion, this walking,
even when we are not walking.

In refuse we find a hidden refusal
to die, a shape

that never forms, a blinking eye
that will not shut.

II

Our parties awkward, our names
stupid, our sex lame, our families

accumulate in the trees their ghosts, buzzards
in the cypress or grackles in the bamboo, to shoot

bottle rockets at. We don't need this shit,
but I'd rather live with racket than divest

my anatomy to a couch. I used to lie
across the tracks, or in weeds

on dry earth. I don't try to sustain
myself by deflecting what returns

its beak to my skull, but survival evolves
ecstasies outside the uses of angels.

I do not dream. I just
watch fields burn, or ride

in cars that won't get anywhere.
I suppose the mind's own place

offers no heaven. I'd rather not slow down,
and I wouldn't shoot a grackle, though

I'd scare the hell out of one, with purpose
and joy. Fear sweet as a fuck

in summer, at a park in the wee hours,
can turn us back to innocence,

bumbling through the real day
while soaring on our wounds.

We are already too far gone to feign
loneliness, too blessed to accept

what surrounds our annihilating impending lack
of doubt, our angel flesh that won't burn.

III

Before I hatchet honeysuckle
and take a pickax to the roots

I embrace the solid and particular
with a mind of glass and broken bricks.

What I become imbues cut brush
with horses and bleak golden ghosts.

Morning does not curse another
morning, but you don't get blessed

for living. You can cut yourself
and not get blessed at all,

but burn your cuttings and imagine
simplified ghosts surrounding

complex horses neighing at the dark,
awake and afraid but not afraid of loss

yet, and not afraid of ghosts ever.
I'm afraid I've become the monstrosity

passing the see-saw,
though not to children,

I'm certain, because my gruesome
eye captures lust

in the green hill, though I stalk
the world like it's an overturned

piss-pot. I'm not
in the pity-pot. I'm hungry

for a new ghost, just under
my wife's breasts,

and the scent of magnolia
where nostalgia was

overcome by honeysuckle cuttings,
my bitter mind broken in fact

because I am not a monster for
seeing the dead living where

we live and where we won't.
A one-hotel skyline blots out

the single cloud on an otherwise
uninspired afternoon. I'm happy

we can get our grief from
the supermarket, the pharmacy,

and the toy store, rather
than having to earn

our pain by fucking up
at a motel on the turnpike.

IV

For complexity or worse, the clustered
knots desire makes our minds undo

betters the dialect of shrubs
and so teaches us to love wholly

the fuck of pain and the doom
of love, which has no place.

I leave the branches to dry
and slip inside, under

the dark, to pour some wine,
and though I don't smoke

I smoke the earth. My bones
have the resin of dirt

and my sore skin peels
and has no place on the linoleum.

Better to lie in bed and die
of idleness than to raise one hand

against my own desire, I say
to no one, because even

my wife would laugh at sadness,
the way I make it mine.

I didn't say I keep
a pasture with some horses

northwest of my medulla oblongata,
but I don't have to.

As I try to sleep, too early
for sleep, a motorcycle

growls off and vanishes,
a mosquito in the dark.

I didn't say I see everything
in the dark, and I'm not inclined

to explain that when I say
"dark" as I nod off I get lost.

I am not inclined to the earth
or to what ruined us or what

we became. I can only say
we cherish ruins.

If I can in the dark,
I look at my forearm,

mistakes made in the woods,
and my busted knee

cracking like water
under a dumb heaven.

Gorge

Fruit in the glass she held in the sink
while looking out the window—

headlights, house—
and thinking inside the tree

ice like a tongue shines, she turned
out all the lights but the dim, lemon bulb.

An ellipse stretched the frame

Light from the garage: hands in the tree.
Memories stopped making sense.

A world living inside
ice around the bark

seemed larger winters
earlier, past light.

Quiet places spun still.
Verboten grass, snow.

The creaking sap broke late
in the tree behind the garage.

Tendons as apertures
shadowed morning's mud.

She felt like flesh. She wasn't hanging.
"All answers are hells."

What she heard about their house dripped from the faucet.
In the morning the tapping and the water filled with light.

A bucket in the garage burned.

Sometimes she'd touch
a body in her empty bed.

A stranger's face, a dark
spot on the wall, watched
her as if from a mirror

and behind the face a hand
held a brush for her hair.

A spider entering a glass
knocked off the table dented the water

Isaac in the desert near a wash
heard the flood in spiders pulsing

First horizon noise
then light sexes afterlife

I slept in a ravine and woke on my carpet
sparrow alit on the tray table

Burning brush on the road
stopped at a train light

I smashed the glass against the door this morning
six birds lifted from the fire escape

there is a sun that feels
and a sun that doesn't

feathers   out in light
                          different music

                    splintering
out there and gone

a feather alit
a lit feather

at the end of the mind before

the sun had wings
the sun has no wings

a fire   a memory   made a sparrow I swallowed
                          spare sorrow

in the spare room made of a cabinet
the glasses glistened

tiny veils

                    wood and cork
                    would listen

                    objects
                    growing fear in the wings

tulips bark   a fire
                                     in a field

          my swallow   my sun
          two suns   tiny veils

                          to listen
                          to tulips bark

                    Walking past
                              tires & ash
                                     broken glass

               feather   fire   field

     city grass   microwave & T.V.

                     as sheep   tulip as dish

                     Brooklyn is anonymous
                     passed walking

                     waking slow
                     never ends

slivers   dish   chain fence   field   Orthodox dome

was ours, the dish, the opening, not the dome, closed, renovating

forgetting   I am

A whale tenderly descends from a star,
another regurgitated sweater on the sidewalk,

fence liberated of bodies
solo swollen-throated coo.

After six the gardens are nothing but brick.
The moon and the broken egg are one.

My box is an empty head, a box of weather,
my hand a box full of zeros.

In the diseased wintering elm a kite
and coo aren't one.

What I erase out here repeats forever.

The New Surrealism

The Seventh Avenue traffic sighs Deus.
We're living in the kingdom of an idea.

Spit in the sewer. This city
sits lower than we know,

Cassandra. This city is
the forest's burning ghost,

the lion's mane, the hushing jowls
Vico sundered with his sword

while Blake, vigilant, dreamed America
out of Saturn, George Washington

throwing the flames back at Hades
and wearing as a cape the Brooklyn Bridge,

designed by Whitman, destroyed by Hart's
short route back to New York

down the Winding Stairs of Liberty
and out of flame, a Pythagorean axiom

enacted: "Don't step over a yoke."
A breath of water for once,

Emerson admonished Ford
and stuck the fork in his own neck.

Out of the ashes, we fought a war
and at the end ate the brains and entrails.

There was a cuckoo in the garden
and, Holly, how we loved entrails.

We took a long time sipping tea,
while an arm of light seemed

this time to reach up to the maple, those fingers,
not the squirrel, tickling your nipple

while you fell in love with Ralph.
I started contemplating suicide

and went to the Hudson everyday
with a sandwich from Murray's.

It was pretty beautiful to be so frail,
and I long for it and even more

for you to long for it. Silence was like
the old music behind the walls.

You were glass. Your shivering was light.
Once a sound made warm, I am not real.

So I woke in a bank, washed my hair with leaves,
donned surrealism for the confidence, and began

to walk among men again. I woke with my face
in the dirt and heard sirens in the silence.

They were everywhere. I was already destroyed.
I saw the rope where I'd had myself strung

to the El. Harlem proposed a landscape
I could not escape. I am now not more

than the red brick above the bar across the street.
Last weekend, I went to see Brancusi at the Guggenheim.

Now everything's wound around that, the dog, her,
loneliness and the trochee, Heidegger and the Rolling Stones.

We're living in a time made clear by the idea
that muddles all thought and mangles the age

of a lion's jowls to a dog's bone. I live
in a studio on West 22nd Street with

my wife, Katy, and last night dreamed
we were back in Wisconsin while the city was nuked.

All we had of Manhattan was an enclosed remote
television station on the New Jersey shore.

And that, my friends, is the New Surrealism.
Out of the ashes, we won't rise. There's Katy,

reading Alfred Döblin, and let me tell you, it is nice,
the silliness we hope to make real, much better

than the actualities we tried to make unreal.
I used to live in Los Angeles and the traffic lights said,

"Move on," and "Juked you," a springtime
of anger in my lily sneakers and crossword puzzles.

Pound said Bunting's definition of poetry ("condensed light")
consisted of more than all the man's creative works. I agree.

When I was reading Basil Bunting I implored him to stop writing.
I lived in my bedroom closet in Gardena, California, and shouted

at Basil Bunting to knock it off. The nervous knocking off!
It was an age of masturbation.

I am not more than light on the brickwork above
the D'Agastino and am the turning across that wall.

I am a blink as blank as the caught fish turning
its eye, or the stones turning always within.

I'm a hive blinding inward, and I'm fire cast through the eyes.
When I look, I see nothing, and when I turn away, I find,

for example, the dumpster behind
the hospital, the asters on the lawn.

I lived in Fayetteville, Arkansas, and learned irony
doesn't work but conceives. There was a Sunday

I stood in the doorway of my apartment
and saw a large cat running in a tree.

That is the old reality. The newer is less
violent to the eyes but more to the body.

There was a Sunday I was blind
drunk and saw the sloshing of myself

in the same tree limb, and hated the breath
of myself, and loved the hatred of self

and all things, and found forgiveness in doing
violence unto my life, and loving my life.

How unbearable for you the tedium of complicity, maybe.

We holidayed in Berlin and slept late. The subway rent our days.
We stayed in a flat with a filmmaker and rolled into bed.

There were sounds on the street. For example, the wall was down
and we were living on many sides of the street at once.

A kid in Prenzlauerberg screamed at us.
We said we were Italians. I broke a beer glass in Prague.

I don't know what to believe. I am robust and sing occasionally,
love horses and the gold within the walls. All the avenues

have shuffled to sleep, and a ceiling fan harries in the window.
I'm the blind beggar of Panama, and God continues snoring

in the wound round us and will until when to be is as was.

Beulah's Rest

NO REALITY BUT THE RUINED IDEA OF
A GOD WE SPEAK TO

Gnat caught in the breath of a dismantled catechism
on a cracked pew in a cathedral by the sea,
restore with your nothing wings
the way to where I left my shoes.

No imagination but in your tiny, ruptured eyes
which may as well see no thing,
before a brain which cannot count,

behind the inverted cradle of my hands,
which in a moment or two
will dispatch what I forget.

DEATH CERTIFICATE

After realizing the angel in the ditch
was my Batman comic torn up

by the lawnmower, I didn't cry.
I wore a blanket for my cape.

Now I sit on the curb as on a dime.
I need the sandwich beat out of me.

When I was hungry I read
an almanac turned into a breast.

I've started over many times.
I hold the door for a stranger

and try to not look at his face.
My shoes mortgaged for a bus ride,

I have killed my brain
with the worm I made a hero.

I pretend the worm but can't feign sleep.
Shall we redeem the violet in a sewer?

THE GOAT

I

I spoke to and fro with the goat I traveled to, or who traveled to me
We do not know these things anymore
We wrote nothing

It was sometimes cool enough in Los Angeles to sit on the concrete
One afternoon the goat and I rested in a drainage ditch
The goat had nothing to say

His speech was somewhat afflicted by a tic
My girlfriend told me he had Asperger's
I think she meant it mean

I preferred the goat to her
She handled objects gently but was mostly vicious
When running away from a vicious person I sometimes forget to run

My feet are clumsy like the goat's
His tic resulted from a physical injury
It is difficult for a goat to find an audience

I consider the tic part of the goat's articulation
The goat related nothing genius nor freakish
I freak hearing you

I have watched the sun about to speak
The sun is no friend
The goat was a man to me

You and I assume
His speech was more convincing than a cat walking on its hind legs
It is easy to yell

II

The goat invented a new form of song

He told me what he heard during the day
He listened closely to what people said

The sun set behind the oil rigs in the evening
I questioned many I called heroes

He sometimes snapped at me when he had nothing to eat
He refused the food I brought him

Gutted immaculate memory
The sun subsumed our modesty

FALLING

Holy tissue made of glass,

my tongue is a flame
you touch with your finger,

a flame I try to swallow, bitter
little bird I am, mother day.

PRISON RECORD

In heaven horseshoes are made of tightly woven horsehair.
When horses die they sleep in the ocean.

When children grow up they divide into their possessions,
and their possessions are invincible.

The first time I saw a gun fired
an older Boy Scout

missed a porcupine in a pine tree
and didn't fire again, though the porcupine

didn't move from the bare spot
on the high branch pointing straight up.

My mind tastes bitter this morning. I'm fortunate
enough, green leaf.

FUCKED UP WORLD

Better present than in any future conceived,
I brought boxes to pack books in.

What can two people make but one bigger loneliness
before falling asleep shoulder to shoulder

in a room of crowded things
the same nameless light hits morning

after merciless morning?
A pile driver in the movie

slams mud until a slum apartment collapses,
Naples in black and white.

Pretend above all to love this thing,
this monstrous idea of a room.

Forget where to put
what and what to give away,

or suggest another corner
worse than the one you know.

FORECAST

Sleep without deceit while morning eye sored
I indulge another monster I'll forget before you wake.

To move above water without mind
in the body injures sentences flogged wrongly.

I don't know how to say I know what's wrong
as noon never nears.

Once we stopped
to see a horse we didn't have to say

what we meant. We didn't have to mean we knew
what neared or where that smear came from

or when it crossed the sky.

APOLOGY FOR A MISERABLE SPRING

Implacable hosts sexed beyond repair
require meaningless

babble, from a stranger, however awkward.
Repair? Break enough you mind no end.

And cordial means worse, unless
in a glass, afterwards smashed.

One religion blesses children with water.
God blessed me with broken glass

this morning on my filthy block.
Last night all words now, even

images reduced to sounds, I don't have to respect
what wasn't, what ever will.

PASSÉ HISTORY TEST

Screwed brain to spine with nut & bolt
but forgot the washer in your pocket.

Make money, dinner & love in the closet
with the closest monkey you can afford.

You love the monkey because you must
obey the law of a desert skull.

Make your river snake. Tail feathers
fake a virile imagination, when every

monkey knows you oblate doom.
Oh happy chance to've made

your life a feature loony tune,
and the gross product, a pearl

of cum on a cactus, does not bloom.

INSOMNIA

I had the busted leg of a plastic chair
to pillow a highway sign's dream.
Once a person on his roof begins to think
about saying fuck you to the particulars,
the only blessing is a stagnant block
in the middle of a dead neighborhood
in a city that has been nowhere since
before you or I were born. And who
and what are we, after words, but
mourners signing a petition at someone's
grave, for better dreams, better meals, better
orgasms, though most of us would rather just
sleep well more often. Jesus, why must it
be so late, so bright and so early?

Ordinary Sun

The Center that Pretends to Start the Engine
Ignores the Regime of Endless Centerlessness.
The Committee for Discovering Purposeless Equations
Rejects the Fixed Necessity of Blissful States.
The Perimeter Dismisses Marginalia.
The Fifth Quarter Earnings Report
Denies the Allegations from the Timeshares Council.

And then there was the need for names. Awareness constituted clearly
of distinctions more serious than spiritual fluency,
                                more blessed than a constituency of warmth.

The body moved above the water
                                and the water was cold.
                                It made the sirens roar.

Chicago. Rubens. Galilee. Genoa. MacBeth.
                                Milton. Sartre. Aaron. God.

We named the cat Delilah. The Hebrew tongue was daylight in Japan,
                        a lightbulb in a Buddhist's bathroom.
Mother was a source without a tongue.

                Center of False Love.

Though each definite person, like a body, was the opposite of an absence.
And absence opposed is the full bloom of love. The metaphor flower
means more than grin at the grime.
                        Which Park. Or the floor.
                        The people-greased floor where no one lives.
When you name the singer forests end.
                        To want the floor that fell through.
Around all these flowers decency rusts
                                because the potential
                                center it consents
                                consumes greased pigs.

The forest is a bold move for the choreographer.
The chorister must row the dishes without a click.
The typist must not let the typewriter fall.
The figure must not sum beyond the possessive.
The boy has his finger in the door.
He is unsure whether the finger or the door is bleeding.
The cat named Alpha (Delilah's twin) licks the fingers on his
    other hand.
The choreographer's son should consider the situation a constraint
on living, perhaps, as baseball is made impossible.
Only in the fields   green fields does the bat still crack.

       The Minister of The Fence.
             let's say
       The Auction Block Atop the Great Pig's Greasy Tail.
       The Functions of Missionaries. The Blistered Field.
       The Mutterer's Opera. Mail Returns. Cold Feet.

The day in the water the pig went blind. The tomato's obligations.
All these busy days we reel away. Orange peels and coffee grounds
and constantly the old country a Saturday afternoon.
To name the singer makes the forest an impossible program.
To name the country blesses the water.
The stick and the snake float
              while the dog sinks endlessly.
              The endless deep lies namelessly
              beneath the creek with many names.

A winter's worth of summer's welter
ran out of the light,
screeched the last sound
and fell.

Because the absent engine cannot cease,
it would not begin to call
the tallest city
tall, would shoulder
the blistered field.
The finger bleeding
would not let go the door.

I live at the end of an alley accessible to repeated alleys
and without end I love. No one must mention this, though
they may admit the light. They may
do whatever the hell they like.

On long evenings
I drink with the walls
and extend down to the docks
and up through the capital markets.
I dance along with a flap
tearing from an awning. The J
in Jacob's Meats. Meager
as a wage. Swift as a thought
on such a cold night. A light
from the bushes. Tomorrow.

A thought-of lake
like a glass flower failed.

Cool mud.
Big fat farmer smokes grace through the braided
hair of a branded pig. The greaseless moon
is the first echo. The door responds with tightness.
The rope hung from the window
does not touch the ground.

At night tar streets run together
like perfect prose.

The new way was getting old. The party started at eleven and everyone came on time. The architect was the only guest. Blind to the colorful settings of the table, he listened to the choreographer's movements, a worn recording that sharpened his wearing memory. A compilation of figures danced on his tongue, but he only knew for certain the numbers behind a feeling as opaque, he was certain, as glass.

Everything is the work of our handicaps.
Soon all spoons make love.

When I came home they were dead. I could not begin to explain any of this but that it occurred at the end of too many alleys. I fingered the door I knew as a boy. The long evening would not end.

When did you learn to weep?
What is the action of the mind?
Where does Hell go?
Why can't we refuse?

The critic's name was Garvey.
Her lateral susurrus
treatise on
the way the young
don't know age.
We'll miss the world bitterly.
We'll go on too long without it.
Et cetera. Without the flashing
eyes we go on. Her nonsense
means noise in the breeding room.
The architect would like a child
who can see. She wants a third
term suicide. Truth is as
obvious as a swallowtail moth
on your finger, boy.

Bitterly the butterfly,
she said. The evening must go on.
Even if Satchel Paige must appear.
Even if Lester Young must solo on a late Billie Holliday recording.
Even if Charlie Parker must never run out of veins.
When R.E. Lee finds the infinite playground.
I am playing chess with Salman Rushdie, damn rules.

Swathed in iron, lost in government,
the critic's history sang reverence to God
of the arbitrary structure, and
each arbitrary structure sang.

The architect wants the story not born yet.

She's choreographing God
in the house
of obliteration.
Which Park is
on the tongue
of no one.

The figured retreat
bleakens the cameras.
This is the house
of no cameras.

Please let that chimera pass. The imaginary dances
so hard it causes
the blister on the son's finger to yield, yellow as the sun can hold.

The evening, in one sense, is over.
Her ironing has control.

Nice story when you're walking away from time, Gary.
Chicago. New Brunswick. Omaha. Richard. Turkey.

Every time is meant.

Past the point of caring, the narrative emerged
as on a highway out of Toledo.
As on a highway out of repeated
claims only the accountant could confirm.
I love everything but money.
And Sonny Liston and Ebbets Field.
To name the culprit and the tragedy
means nothing until our hands
are full of blood and we drink from them like it's orange juice.
I love the way metaphor can corrupt
but so seldom allow it.
Though each allowance is
an interruption.
I sing loud enough.

When she came to the curb
I held out my paper cup.